THE POWER OF TRYING

FINDING YOUR SUCCESS

MAURICE JOHNSON

EDITED BY
KAREN SUE REDLACK

A SelfPublishMe Book

THE POWER OF TRYING, Finding Your Success
Copyright © 2019, Maurice Johnson All rights reserved. No part of this book may be used or reproduced in any manner without written permission from the author, except in the case of brief quotations embodied in articles and reviews.

ISBN - 9781095482001

Edited by Karen Sue Redlack

Book cover design and interior layout provided by **SelfPublishMe** *Publishing Consulting and Book Design Services for Independent Authors.* www.selfpublishme.com email: info@selfpublishme.com or selfpublishme@gmail.com

DEDICATION

To my brother, Sepphoris Johnson, whose endless energy, motivation and determination remained aflame no matter what adversities were before him.

CONTENTS

Dedication	iii
Acknowledgments	vi
Prologue	vii
Introduction	ix
A Statement Of Empowerment	xii
Why I Wrote This Book	xiv
What This Book Is About	xvii

CHAPTER ONE: 18
It All Starts With An Initial Spark

CHAPTER TWO: 38
All This Talk Of Success

CHAPTER THREE: 48
Find Your Purpose, Enrich Your Life

CHAPTER FOUR: 70
Mastering Your Destiny

CHAPTER FIVE: 87
Three Of My Success Milestones, An Inside Look

Closing Thoughts	109
About The Author	110

ACKNOWLEDGEMENTS

I want to express my gratitude to my family, ambitious friends and acquaintances with whom I've had many deep conversations over cup after cup, and more cups of coffee. To all the dreamers of the world with a burning desire and motivation to achieve.

PROLOGUE

It strikes me as odd, but at times it seems as if I've become the embodiment of my older brother, Sepphoris—to whom this book is dedicated, bestowing hope and inspiration as friends and sometimes strangers share with me their dreams, goals and aspirations. I would often tell Sepphoris, *"Man, you have the mind of a millionaire!"* He could never stop thinking of how to get some new idea off the ground. There was hardly a business venture that didn't interest him, as he'd expound well beyond the initial concept, picking it apart, analyzing every opportunity to take an idea even further. It was a truly amazing gift he had. Our last conversation was of business. From his hospital bed, curled up in a morphine induced sleep, he had awakened as my good friend and former business partner, James Dale and I entered his hospital room. Insisting that we stay, Sepphoris knew that James and I were in the beginning stages of a new business venture and quickly grew quite alert. His eagerness to engage in a business dialogue was profoundly evident as a light came into his eyes. In those few short moments he went from a feeble patient in a single bed hospital room, laying in a fetal position to a fully alert and excited, fast talking business consultant. It was amazing to see. It was as if Sepphoris actually needed this.

INTRODUCTION

A touch of motivation is good for the soul, and a lot is even better. —MAURICE JOHNSON

The Power of Trying should serve as fuel that perpetually motivates your desire to achieve—your drive, or whatever it is that burns deep within you as you live, not simply to exist, but to succeed.

I do what I do because I'm motivated. Many years ago, a flame was ignited in me and has remained lit to this very day, despite times of adversity and indecision. As we explore the parallels of success, motivation and the power of trying, I can only cite to you the accounts of my own achievements, but nonetheless, they serve as a demonstration in self-motivation, self-belief and determination. I encourage you to aspire to be a better version of you than the day before, and every day moving forward. Aspire to move beyond the boundaries of preconceived limitations.

If the concept of this motive is not yet within you, adopt it now as a core principal or personal philosophy to build upon. Live by it and watch yourself grow, transforming yourself from a dreamer to a doer. For the most part these are the primary talking points within this book. As you make your way from topic to topic there may be something that rings a chord within you. In the hopes of helping you find those pivotal, earth shattering, ground breaking, I BELIEVE I CAN DO THIS points in your life. It doesn't matter how basic or minuscule one's ambitions may seem, there's value in what you do. At the core of every idea, inspiration and ambition are the initial sparks that set it all into motion. Once that spark is lit, what happens next may not reveal itself to you with finite clarity, but much like the gestation period of any living thing, it's destined to come forth. However, to what degree remains to be tested, contingent on a host of factors that all center around you, your frame of mind and of course, let's not forget, motivation.

I really believe that inspiration can be infectious. Reason why, because over the years I've come across a number of enterprising individuals engaged in a variety of ambitious endeavors. At some point in the conversation I'm thrown into the role of motivational coach, consulting yet another knowledge hungry soul desperately in need of direction and enlightenment. Perhaps it's my own innate awareness that leads me down this path time and time again, but after it's all said and done, that individual is visibly energized with a renewed sense of interest, self-empowerment, gratitude and inspiration.

As you become more engaged in pursuing an idea, find an advocate who's in your corner. Believe me, you'll need someone like that along the way.

A Statement Of Empowerment

I like to start many of my books with a statement of empowerment, so this one is no different.

I want to tell you something right now. Maybe some of you need to know what comes out of your mind is worthy, qualifiable and has value. When I say value, I'm not speaking of monetary value, but rather the value of legitimacy. Your thoughts, your words, your creations, your actions. Whatever they may be, it's important for you to know, they are just as important and significant as anyone else's. At the moment, *you* are the most important person in the room.

THE POWER OF TRYING isn't just a title I dreamed up to grace the cover of this book. It is a true statement of self-empowerment, one that I want you to know about and live by throughout your journey to motivation and success. Call it what you will, a subtle push, an inspiring word, a vote of confidence. The fact remains, something as simple as a few sincere, well meaning words can have a profound impact on an individual for the rest of his life. It happened for me and it can happen for you.

I'll admit, life can overshadow what once were dreams, leaving some to settle for an existence of unrewarding complacency, while the boundaries of their full potential remain untested. Sometimes all it takes is for someone else to see the potential in you and say, *"You can do that!"* and then something clicks and you're on your way.

Keep This In Mind

This is YOUR book! Don't baby it. Crack it open, dog ear the pages and read it. In fact, I suggest you have a highlighter handy, and if you see something that catches your eye or grabs your attention, *highlight it* so you can come back to it whenever you'd like.

Why I Wrote This Book

Just like many of my other books, I wrote THE POWER OF TRYING because I live some aspect of it every single day. True, the title pretty well defines me, and as you continue reading, you'll get a better glimpse of who I am and what drives me. That being said, I'm often in the company of someone struggling with a goal, aspiration or idea that's been deterred by fear, a lack of knowledge, resources, confidence, sheer motivation or a host of other things. THE POWER OF TRYING, *Finding Your Success* encompasses all of these. In the midst of adversity and self-doubt, the fire that burns within you is sometimes the only thing that will carry you through. Although the bulk of my previous books center around aspects of music and performance as a business, at their core the message is firmly steeped in motivation, encouragement and advocacy. This book, devoid of music and related business connotations was inspired by the very same core principles and concepts surrounding motivation, encouragement and advocacy. Needless to say, the target audience is vastly general and quite broad, yet it was specifically written to speak directly to *you*. Year after year the idea has been persistently compelling and further validated as friends and acquaintances routinely offered up the suggestion, so here it is. I've done many things over the years and from the standpoint of motivation, I knew it was time to share my insights and experiences. So many times someone would say, "Maurice, you ought to be a motivational speaker, marketing consultant or teach a course." It's always flattering and encouraging to hear, but I guess in a way, I've been and done them all. Unofficially perhaps, but to those who needed it at the time, I played the role. Conviction, passion and exuberance was the typical tone of my dialogue during each of these one-on-one mentoring moments. It was the accumulation of ambitious endeavors, past achievements and a stream of isolated impromptu sessions I've conducted over the years that convinced me to write this book. In the back of my mind I keep telling myself, there has to be something to this, a connection. Not only do mentoring experiences occur over and over again, but I enjoy them just as much as playing guitar, art or any other avid interest that grabs my attention. As an artist, musician, dreamer and chronic multitasker at heart, every step of the way, ambition has driven me to try many new things, even small roles in film and television commercials. Can you imagine that? I would never be complacent with a status quo, mediocre lifestyle. Although my ambitions can outpace me at times, no sooner completing one project before moving to the next, on my list of unexplored challenges. It took me a while to get here—to where I am now. I view it as a clean slate of sorts. One that has nothing to do with Maurice Johnson the jazz guitarist, the artist, the writer or entrepreneur, and yet it has everything to do with all of them and more. This is for the everyday person, entrepreneur, artist, writer, musician, business minded, life-living and self-discovering dreamer in you.

THE POWER OF TRYING is my response to close friends and associates who eagerly asked me questions, listened and kept on asking over the years. THE POWER OF TRYING is for those whose reawakened zeal, new-found courage and brilliant ideas whispered to you in your dreams and screamed to you out loud in your waking hours.

What This Book Is About

THE POWER OF TRYING is about energizing your efforts and becoming empowered through self-belief and motivation. It's about moving forward, staving off fear, self-doubt, procrastination, uncertainty and confusion.

It's about how to find inspiration, motivation and self-worth and applying it to your day to day thinking, including personal or business endeavors, whatever they may be. THE POWER OF TRYING is about moving the ball in your court and placing the world in your favor.

For a slightly different take on this concept, you could also view it as a motivational piece that focuses on breaking through the fear of success and failure while pursuing life goals, no matter what they are. I can certainly tell you this isn't a book about starting a business or how to bring a product to market. It's about moving you into action and placing yourself in the pathway of opportunity, creating your own opportunities, gaining your inner strength and confidence as you build a unique timeline of new experiences and personal success milestones.

CHAPTER ONE

IT ALL STARTS WITH AN INITIAL SPARK

The tragedy isn't the act of being denied an opportunity. It's the act of not creating one.
—MAURICE JOHNSON

The very idea of man-made fire was born from a spark, when two flint stones were struck together among a tuft of dry twigs. Those first few attempts weren't easy, and quite physically demanding at that, but what resulted would change the world forever.

So, what does that have to do with you, motivation and success? It's simple, your journey starts right here, with the energy and effort you put into creating your initial spark. It all depends on the power within *you*.

Life is a demonstration in inspiration, motivation and determination. Sometimes we have to fight to keep these in place, because without them any measure of success, gratification or sense of achievement may never be realized. Starting at this very moment, you must ignite your flame and keep it lit. Your flame, your inner flame in this instance, is the fire that burns deep within you. Some refer to it as drive, will, determination, sticktoitiveness, persistence or motivation. Throughout this book I refer to them all, equally and interchangeably as we explore the power within you and how it relates to igniting *your* flame and finding success through motivation.

First Things First

It's important to realize you're responsible for your own first steps, and no one can make them for you. Having said that, I must acknowledge, reading this is an undeniable testament to your determination to put yourself in charge and make your own choices, no matter what.

Everything you need to move forward is already within you. No one has to qualify you, or grant you the authority to believe in yourself. That is a power that you, and you alone possess. All you have to do is know it, acknowledge it, and live it. Congratulations! You are on your way.

Strength And Motivation.
Where Does It Come From?

Your strength and motivation are the result of unyielding determination. We all have the capacity to summon it within us, but there must be a purpose or goal in place. It silences the voice of fear, and it's your greatest combatant of failure. Your own determination is the driving force behind immeasurable strength and motivation, pushing you beyond what seems impossible.

The rewards are your ability to complete an objective, thus allowing you to swiftly move on to the next. Monetary gains, if that's your desire, may seem slow in coming but it can happen. You're rich with ideas, and best of all, you're able and willing to put them into action.

A Word To The Young Mother Who Says, "You Can't Be Anything When You're A Single Parent"

I didn't dream up this topic. It was actually spoken to me by a young mother. It was such a profound sentiment, I had to include it in this book.

True, motherhood comes before anything else, but it's not all that you are. You are a woman of great substance, filled with amazing potential, who just happens to be a mother as well. Repeat that back to yourself if you need to, and let it sink in for a while. That's what you must ALWAYS remember! Don't let motherhood become an excuse to throw your dreams in the closet, never to be seen again.

I really understand the scope and responsibilities of parenthood. Things may not move as fast as we want them to with a family in tow. Hold on to your ambitions. Pace yourself, and NEVER stop dreaming. The same goes for working fathers, young and old, or anyone barely making ends meet.

Don't Get Heated Up About Age

It doesn't matter. I'll preface this by saying, live life and forget about your age. Don't ever think that life has passed you by. The truth of the matter is, your mind or *mindset* in this case would likely play a greater role regarding the lack of motivation or forfeited opportunities long before your age ever will. Starting your journey toward your future successes begins with your belief that it's possible. Whatever it is, you must firmly believe in it and sincerely want it. The same school of thought also applies when it comes to thinking with an old mind. *(As if you're much older than you really are.)* Often I'll come across someone whose mindset is advanced in years well beyond their chronological age. For whatever reason they've placed an early expiration date on dreams, goals and ambitions. You're not too old. In fact, it's *your* time. Embrace it, own it, rule it! Surely you've heard the term, *late bloomer*. If age is a factor of concern for you, so be it. With that being said, put it aside and move on. In the absence of debilitating physical limitations, all you have to do now is believe that you can, earnestly want it and be motivated enough to get started.

It still astonishes me when someone says they once had ambitions, and now feel that time for ambitions and dreams has passed them by. Let me tell you, unless you're gravely ill or now deceased, you still have time. If you have a sound mind and willing faculties, you're not too old to have dreams, and you're never too old to have ambitions, *youthful* ambitions at that. I can only assume, if you're living with this mindset, you're just looking for an easy out while you keep telling yourselves, *"I'll just continue doing what I've always been doing and dare not pursue a dream."* Listen, you're going to have to take it upon yourself to start from where you are *right now* in life. Don't worry about all the time you feel you've wasted. Your tomorrows begin today. If the regrets of your yesterdays are looming over your head, you *must* debunk them at this very moment. They don't count. If it will help you to move forward, you will have to disqualify them and not allow yesterday to infringe on your tomorrow. I agree, no one or anything can dismiss the fact that a part of who you are is the product of your yesterdays. Nonetheless, at times it may become an absolute necessity to quiet the negative noise, detracting moments and the most confining events of your past. Grant yourself the right to become upwardly mobile and gainfully ambitious. Starting today, you must put your yesterdays behind you. Once you've done that, leave them there, and never allow them to become a convenient point of refuge or a pillar to stand behind anytime your confidence is challenged. Don't use your yesterdays as an excuse to fail or falter in your efforts toward obtaining your goals. From this point forward, it's only you, today and tomorrow. Start from where you are right now and don't look back.

Aspire To Be Something - Aspire To Do Something

No matter how small it is or insignificant it may seem to others, you must want it bad enough to work for it and sometimes even live for it.

Today, your new life begins, but I want you to understand and appreciate the fact that everyone has their own individual starting point. So don't be distracted by those within your personal sphere who have resources, skill sets or specific knowledge that is currently beyond your own. This is the time when you must focus on *you*, first and foremost. As you work from your individual starting point, you will sometimes need to put blinders on. I'm not talking about real, physical blinders, but mental blinders to block all the distractions going on around you. There is no room for jealousy and envy of those who are trying to better themselves, just like you. In other words, work with what you've got. Your earnest efforts toward your personal aspirations is not a competition. Don't subject yourself to undue stress to impress someone.

Feel good about who *you* are. Feel good about the abilities, knowledge, the raw desire and determination that *you* have. Recognize that you are important to someone, and just as importantly, to yourself. Wear your strength on the outside whenever you can, even if you can never speak about it.

I want you to try something. Not for me, but for you. When you get out of bed in the morning, I want you to walk in the bathroom and close the door behind you. Now, look into the mirror and say to that person, *"I believe in you."* Do this everyday, until you really believe it. Don't be afraid to expound on the idea. Say to that person, "You're intelligent. Your thoughts, opinions and ideas matter, and what you don't know, you can learn."

You must be determined to live life, no matter what. You must exist and think with an enterprising and curious mind. Even more, you must become an enterprise within yourself. So what if you don't drive the latest model car. So what if you don't own a home. So what if your credit score isn't where you'd like it to be right now. With an enterprising mind, you can formulate a plan of action to take yourself anywhere you want.

What Is Your Calling In Life?

It may come as no surprise, but a lot of people can't answer this fundamental yet vital question.

Oddly enough, while writing this book, it was during a phone conversation when a good friend asked me that very same question, point blank. I didn't expect it and to be quite honest, it caught me off guard, totally. Much to my embarrassment, I couldn't answer it at that moment. *What is your calling in life?* Hmmm, it was one of those menacing, inescapable questions that demanded an answer. I've pondered it myself throughout the years.

To this day I wrestle with the definitive answer because I've done so many things and I know I wouldn't be happy just doing one of them. Whatever my own calling is in life, I've never believed it to be centered around just one single solitary thing, but having thought on it, that appears to be the case—at least partially. Having said all that, I've come to the conclusion that *my* calling in life at it's core centers around motivation. Yep, that's it, *motivation*. The majority of the public know me as a jazz guitarist/author, but those closest to me, know me as a husband, father, grandparent, dreamer, optimist and chronic motivator. Music is only a part of my life and in no way does it define the totality of who I am. My goals, objectives and desires are quite varied. One thing I do know is, it drives my wife crazy. She insists, the scope of my constant conceptualizing, ideas, interests and projects tend to overwhelm her, but over the years she's come to accept the cacophony of creative chaos that spews from my mind almost daily.

Action Vs. Opportunity

Opportunity can be the lifeblood of your success milestones, and your actions will play a direct role in how they come about. Consider this. An opportunity will present itself whether you had a hand in it or not, whereas an action, or the effort you put forth cultivates potential for new opportunities that may not have occurred otherwise. Rather than waiting for an opportunity to happen, you must place yourself in the pathway of opportunity by your continued determination, persistence and gainful actions.

Make The Change From A Dreamer To A Doer

You may have heard the phrase, "change the way you think and it will change your life."

Well, guess what? It's true, and to be perfectly honest, it doesn't get any simpler than that. Maybe you've been in a job for the past several years and the only reward, sense of purpose or accomplishment is making a car payment, paying the mortgage, keeping the lights on and maybe a movie or dining out once or twice a month. I know many of you can relate to this, all the while, living a life that's typical of many, neatly confined to a well worn and beaten path of predictability. If you're ever going to make the move from a dreamer to a doer you will first need to change the way you think. Even more, I suggest you change your daily routine and take an alternate path in your decision making and actions. Visualize where you want to be in life and start taking steps in that direction. It's *your* time now. It's time to stop wishing and start doing.

A *Wish* A *Dream* and A *Goal,* Here's The Difference.

They may seem similar, but each one conveys its own distinctly unique connotation.

1. A *wish*, no matter how sincere, is momentary and fleeting at best, lacking in determination and drive to facilitate its realization.

2. A *dream* is an intuitive vision that one can act upon in order to bring it to fruition.

3. A *goal* is an established objective set with the express intention of achieving it.

Pick two that best applies to you.

Overcome Excuses To Fail

Nothing troubles me more than the restrictions and limitations we put on ourselves. So I must confess, this is strictly a passion driven statement, and I mean this with all that is within me.

You must *always* place your mind beyond what you perceive as physical limitations. It costs nothing to think beyond your bank account, mortgage, car payment, utility bills, etc. To dream and imagine is absolutely free. Don't let anything including your own pragmatic mind work against you.

It's Time To Follow Your Own Dreams

Whose dreams are you going to follow, yours or someone else's? Whose ideas will flourish in your mind, take root and spawn into something far greater than you originally imagined? Your mind is not a docile conduit to process everyone else's creative genius, other than your own and its certainly not a disposal ground for idle and useless input. It is a working, thinking and brilliant machine that was designed exclusively for you and all that you create within your power of thought. Yours is the genius mind that orchestrates the use of it's own content that best facilitates your interests, aspirations, goals and objectives.

You must never allow anyone, or anything to usurp the power and command of your own original thought. Now, more than ever, it's time to follow the dreams that are born of your own mind with strict confidence and matter-of-factness.

So, Whats Your Dream?
- Write a book
- Bring a product to market
- Become a business owner
- An inventor
- An entertainer
- A public speaker
- An artist
- Buy your first home
- Become a real estate investor
- An actor
- A community leader
- An influencer
- A consultant
- Weight loss and better health
- Be happy
- A better you than you were yesterday

These are all realistic and purposeful goals that can enrich your life, state of being and overall sense of achievement. All you have to do is find *your* purpose.

Get Fired Up!

From the outset, as you strive to ignite your inner flame, at times it will require that you come out swinging just to get started. It's understandable that everyone is different with their own set of circumstances, level of will and determination. Just know and be prepared when life leans on you a bit and demands that you fight your way through the starting gate—get fired up and be the warrior that you are!

I won't deny that depression is real and debilitating at times. Early morning bouts of depression can rob us of our day and most productive hours. Before you know it you're still in bed, consumed by the same feeling you woke up with earlier that morning. If you can defeat the urge to remain in bed and do nothing, at all costs, *do so!*

Here's another scenario. You're at home, sitting at the dining room table or in front of your computer with a stack of bills and a couple of cutoff notices for good measure. Currently you work for yourself and your pay cycle doesn't correlate with the constant flow of monthly utility bills, mortgage payments, car payments, credit card payments, insurance payments, cell phone bill payments, I believe you get the picture. But this time you're in the middle of writing a book, planning a career move, or simply surviving. Yes, life can be tough at times, and I understand for some, it can be tougher than others. But these are the times when you're doing your level best trying to maintain, we have to become warriors. I don't say this lightly. At times it's going to take that fighting spirit just to make it through the day, and the next day, and the next. The fact is, it can only come from within *you*.

During your most challenging and leanest of times, don't stop dreaming. Don't stop planning. Don't stop believing. But whatever you do, if during these times, you're engaged in a project, e.g. developing a business idea or product, or simply trying to orchestrate a way to get through your current situation, DON'T STOP! You must keep moving, conceptualizing, discussing, producing, writing, keep your mind and wits about you, but most of all, keep believing.

Explore Your Potential And Test Your Boundaries

Exploring your own self-potential and testing the limits of your boundaries is a worthy, lifelong endeavor of notable mention. Needless to say and much to your own benefit, be tenacious, driven, unwavering and unapologetic in your desire to do so. True, life will at times offer up some of its most unfavorable moments. Stay curious, ask questions, discover and explore. It's not a matter of where life can take you but rather, where you can take life, while never allowing yourself to become the docile victim of a painfully predictable and mundane existence. Keep telling yourself, *"It's my story and this is how I'm going to write it!"*. Take a moment and look around.

You may determine it's time to realize a dream that's been waiting in the wings over the years. Perhaps you've raised a family, worked through the span of a career, or reached the proverbial glass ceiling. Could it be a reawakened yearning that relentlessly beckons your attention to your calling, your purpose perhaps? Whatever it may be, don't hold back. Go about your ambitions with a healthy dose of vigor, heart and soul, promise and passion. Allow yourself to get lost in the moments of inspiration, in the days of creativeness and in the years of unyielding pursuit. Whether you realize it or not, every single day will bring you closer to your next desired goal. Your only requirement is, you'll have to want it bad enough. With all of this in mind, I reiterate my opening statement, "Explore your potential and test your boundaries."

These are just a few of your super powers.

The power of	*Ideas*
The power of	*Enthusiasm*
The power of	*Passion*
The power of	*Creativity*
The power of	*Courage*
The power of	*Knowhow*
The power of	*Understanding*
The power of	*Tenacity*
The power of	*Patience*
The power of	*Reawakening*
The power of	*Interest*
The power of	*Curiosity*
The power of	*Self-empowerment*

CHAPTER TWO

ALL THIS TALK OF SUCCESS

*A margin of success is measured by
your perception of success.*
—MAURICE JOHNSON

Do You Know What Success Is? All this talk of success and how to obtain it holds a significant degree of merit and relevance. It is the life-long pursuit of those who hunger for it, and the quiet disappointment for those who feel they will never achieve it. Success for the most part is the skilled art of perception. As basic as it sounds, *knowing* what success is, is critical to your pursuit of success. Bottom line, if you can't define it, you can't have it. If you don't know where it is, and how to find it, how are you going to get there? This is an important school of thought to consider and live by throughout all of your endeavors. Many have an idea of what they perceive success to be, no matter how misguided or superficial in some cases. Lots of friends/*social network followers*, lots of money, popularity, a nice car or home, etc. Perhaps some of these may very well be what you envision as success, and that's okay. Success can be both simple and complex. No matter what ultimately defines *your* idea of success, it will require a series of smaller successes—success milestones to get there. Society tends to push wealth, or financial prosperity as the biggest qualifier of success. I'm of the opinion that success should be painted with a broader brush, broken down into smaller increments, or success milestones as I mentioned earlier. We'll cover success milestones further in a bit.

Why You Should Thank Failure For Your Successes

With the right attitude you can turn failures into future successes, and negatives into positives. When it comes down to it, it's all a matter of how you look at it. Failure is nothing more than an opportunity. Over the years, during a job interview, or some type of evaluation, a particular question would often come up. It went something like this, as I'd sit at a desk or some long conference table just across from my interviewer. *"What motivates you?"*, or *"Where do you get your motivation?"* I'd always give the same response. I don't know where it came from. It just seemed the most truthful and natural thing to say. My response went something like this. *"Failure… I'm motivated by failure."* I could always tell, no one was ever prepared to hear that response. Their reaction was usually a simple one word statement, with a bit of a curious tone to it. *"Really"*, they'd say. It was never inflected as a question, but merely a single word statement. They'd follow-up the question, *"How does failure motivate you?"* My answer was simply, *"Because it makes me know I can do better."* All of your failures, or what you may perceive as failure should never be viewed as damning or erosive to your confidence or determination. These events, episodes or experiences, if you will, are nothing more than lessons from which to learn, and at the same time, improve your odds of destined successful outcomes. Once you finally arrive at anticipated success points you will have matured, bringing a renewed sense of tempered awareness, confidence and strategic knowhow to future endeavors. What you might perceive as failure is simply the ticket you bought to get to where it is you're going.

The Road To Success Is Motivation

Rarely is success an accidental occurrence. A lot can go on behind the scenes before an idea becomes an endeavor, then ultimately an achievement. Given everyone's individual circumstances the likelihood of being met with stumbling blocks along the way is a realistic possibility. Whether physical, financial or the simple lack of knowledge, the most critical yet basic ingredient to any form of success is the motivation to obtain it. At times you may need to double down in your efforts to stay motivated, because without it, nothing will happen. Your success will depend on you and the drive you put behind every endeavor. Whatever it takes, keep your focus. Put your emotional blinders on when necessary, and surround yourself with energized and motivated people.

5 Steps To A Successful Beginning

1. *Be Ambitious And Believe In Yourself*

If you truly want to ignite your flame and keep it lit, you're going to need a good amount of ambition and a strong sense of self-belief. Neither of these can be taught, or bestowed upon you by someone else, but those around you can become influential factors, both positive and negative. I'm sure there have been many debates that support the idea of environment and positive interaction as influential factors. These are qualities that are deep within all of us, which may or may not be triggered at some point in our lives. Your self-belief can outweigh occasions when affirmations are slow to come or things don't appear to be moving in the same direction that you are.

Like the law of motion, ambition can be defined as *the law of motivation*—that perpetual spirit that fuels the hearts of ambitious thinkers. That includes you.

2. *Be Persistent*

No matter how overwhelming things may seem at times, persistence will eventually offer gratifying rewards, because sooner or later someone will react in your favor because of it. Persistence will take you through each phase of your moving forward and breaking out of the shell of self-imposed doubt. It will take you through greater achievements yet to come. In the academic world, students are classified in two categories, *achievers* and *non-achievers*. For the so-called non-achiever, rather than a limited intellectual capacity, the lack of persistence is often the contributing factor that separates the two.

3. Know Your Strongest Skill Sets

In a word, learn to identify attributes that you already possess. Believe me, you have many. Some of you will need to look deeper to recognize and clearly see just how qualified you really are. It's there, and you should never stop looking for it. At this point, it's very important that you are fully aware of your strongest, qualifiable attributes and abilities. You must earnestly believe, right now, that you have the strength, skills and ability to move past what you may perceive as limitations.

4. Organize Your Thoughts

Get into the habit of making a daily *to do* list for the following day, listing only tasks that can realistically be accomplished within the course of a day. It's important to follow through with each one before moving on to the next. If this isn't already a part of your daily routine, try it for a month and watch your productivity and rate of success increase. It all boils down to developing a sense of organized thought and following through to completion.

5. Set Deadlines

In essence, deadlines are nothing more than a series of short-term goals set with the intention of completing each task within a specified timeline. When you set deadlines and meet them on time, your productivity will steadily increase along with your personal efficiency.

You can apply the following steps to enhance your own personal productivity and meet established deadlines:

- Routinely write a list of upcoming projects.

- Number the items in your list, arranging them in order of importance and including deadlines for each. (Be sure to give yourself realistic time constraints).

- Decide, *(only when necessary)* which projects can be rescheduled for a later date.

- Starting with the highest-priority item, complete each one before moving to the next.

The key to meeting deadlines is not to overwhelm yourself with too many projects at once. Organization will play a critical role in your overall rate of success. With no established goals or realistic deadlines, your productivity is at risk of a virtual standstill with success milestones *very* slow in coming.

What Does Your Success Look Like?

Can you see yourself as successful? Can you describe what your success actually looks like? Whatever it is you aspire to do, you must be able to see yourself as successful in it. In your mind's eye, you must place yourself in the picture of success. See it, taste it, smell it. You must inundate yourself with the idea and vivid intention of achieving your desired goals. Visualizing your own success will help you understand, the power of possibility can greatly exceed the potential of improbability. It is with this understanding you can make your successes happen. The vantage point from which you perceive as true is the reality that is destined to be, so I ask again, what does your success look like?

CHAPTER THREE

FIND YOUR PURPOSE, ENRICH YOUR LIFE

Although mysteries abound within the conscious mind, the subconscious mind holds the answers.
—MAURICE JOHNSON

Your life has purpose. Do you know what it is? Deeply ingrained in the topic of motivation and moving past your limitations, knowing what your purpose is in life. It is as critical as breathing. If you're ever going to move forward to achieve the dreams, hopes and desires that you deserve, knowing your purpose will be the key to reaching the apex of your abilities. If you were to place five people in a room together, give them a single, complex task with multiple variables that requires a team effort in order to solve it, what do you think it would reveal? Although they're all trying to work as a unit, individual processes would likely form before a collective concept and a subsequent effort can begin. Given enough time or attempts, one would likely begin to notice that each team member brings their unique set of skills and abilities.

Knowing What Your Purpose Is Early On

Some will ask, is it really this simple to do what comes natural? The greatest defeaters of knowing your purpose is not doing what comes natural to you. So many individuals go through years of education and training to secure a career or job they don't enjoy at all, subsequently enduring it for years, with no real sense of purpose. For the majority, life's working model has been to find a job that brings an income in order to make a living. We have been conditioned to seek out, live and sustain the rest of our natural lives on that path. It doesn't matter if it's something we enjoy. There are those who surrender to the idea, the capacity in which they serve at their job defines their purpose. Some cling to the philosophy, do what you do best and stick with it.

Put Your Heart Into Everything You Do

If your purpose deviates from your realm of interest, your heart won't be in it.

Based on that alone, effort, enthusiasm, motivation all wane and struggle to survive.

In reality, your heart is what drives your passion and ambitions, which in turn, will ultimately fuel your purpose.

You May Already Be Living Your Purpose Without Realizing It

Following the path of what you're good at and pursuing a passion driven idea that's outside the realm of your skill set are clearly two different channels of thinking. It's a distinction that yields to the perception of one who is considered a jack of all trades or a born natural in multiple extraordinarily different areas of expertise.

Life's purpose is not always in plain sight or clearly marked like a traffic sign illuminating in your headlights just up ahead. Sometimes purpose has to find you. In reality a great number of individuals go through an entire lifetime never knowing their purpose, or calling as some would say. Even more surprising, there are those who are totally oblivious to the concept that life has a purpose beyond that of simple day to day, commonly shared realities. Personally, I've never subscribed to the idea that the hallmark of our existence and ultimate destiny be rigidly defined by a job, family and just paying a sequential chronology of bills every month, yet a fair amount of the population cling to the notion this is what life is all about. Needless to say, if you're a complacent individual, content with where you are within a predefined template of where you will be, it may be the case after all if that's what your heart and mind tells you. Having said that, I want you to know and understand, don't run from your purpose when it taps you on the shoulder. Much of the time, you may not be aware of it when it seeks you out or drops a hint every now and then, *"Maybe you ought go in this direction."* For example, more often than not you're the designated go-to person empowered to resolve a unique situation or facilitate a service because you possess a specific and above average level of understanding in a particular area.

Somewhere within you is encoded an innate ability to fill a need, or a range of needs with a consistent and accelerated rate of success among a majority of those you come in contact with. More importantly, what ever it is, you go about it with a great sense of passion and drive. It's as if you feel it is something that you *must* do, and when you're not doing it you distinctly feel a void. If this describes you, it's a strong possibility your purpose is trying to get your attention. The decision to accept and embrace it is yours to make, but you must first recognize it when it calls to you.

To Ignite Your Flame, You Must Have A Goal

Without goals, no amount of motivation, regardless of the source, including family, friends, strangers, or even this book can effectively serve its purpose. In other words, you must have a desire to achieve something. Without an initial desire and drive, nothing will happen. Nothing *can* happen. There is however, potential, until a goal is established.

Has it ever occurred to you that everything in life derives from an initial action based on a predetermined purpose and goal? As we go about our busy, day-to-day lives, I'd venture to say, rarely, if at all do we give the idea any thought, but nonetheless these are two primary contingencies that lie at the very core of our personal progress and rate of personal achievement. It's not a hypothesis or an ambitious unproven theory. The fact that you and I, and everything around us even exists is evidence that life and all that is in it, is the product of an initiated action built upon a purposeful goal. It was a single sperm that swam in a sea of tremendous improbably among a million others, at the risk of an impending fate that set out on a purposeful goal to fertilize an egg. My hope with this analogy is to give you a visual to help you understand the point I'm trying to make. I don't want to sound like a philosophy major attempting to unravel the meaning of life, but once you've digested this concept, you might begin to realize how profound it really is.

What's most intriguing about this is, you can have a goal and not know your purpose. That's not to say that reaching a goal isn't possible without first realizing your purpose, or vice versa. In the absence of realizing your purpose or calling in life, one can likely find themselves on a scattered and inconsistent path to personal gratification.

Be True To Your Passion

I'm not immune to offers of joining some amazing new multilevel marketing program. In fact, its been a reoccurring theme for me over the years.

Typically I'll run into someone at a restaurant, coffee shop a retail store or the like, after a brief dialogue… I'd politely say, thank you for the opportunity, but in all fairness to you, I wouldn't be true to it. In the past it was always difficult for me to just say, I'm not interested before they'd begin ramping up their sales pitch and attempt to reel me in with a commitment to sign up for an even more aggressive recruitment campaign. It's not where my passion lies. For those ambitious recruiters, it can be a challenging argument to counter. All I'm saying is, you have to have enough faith in your own personal passions, not answering the call to everyone else's prefabricated, *make me rich* marketing ideas. I've had friends who'd chase casinos, not just for entertainment, but in hopes of winning that big payoff as another paycheck disappears. It's a broken and fragmented dream, upon which someones faith is built.

Your Intent To Succeed *Must* Be Greater Than Your Fear Of Failing

I won't qualify success and failure as a delicate balancing act. In my mind, they are opposing adversaries that must reside within their own, isolated realm. I'd prefer to view them as cut and dry, black or white, with no grey area in between. Pick one... you decide. Refuse one and pick the other. With the proper mindset, it will be totally your call, not someone else's or a particular set of circumstances of which you have no controls. This is *your* destiny we're talking about. No one has the right to impose. One must be far removed from your mind.

No Matter What, You Must Become A Versatile Thinker

Our brains and minds are in a constant state of readiness, calculating and negotiating our every thought, and all the while, reserving the startling ability to readjust its calculations in an instant. While still a great mystery to us and the worlds most accomplished scientific and medical minds, this is what gives us all the ability to process our most complex thoughts and corresponding course of action. In this very same vein, it's important that you employ this amazing capacity of your brains ability and never allow yourself to become static and inflexible in your thinking. Throughout your life there will be times when it becomes necessary to shift your thinking as you make your way toward an ultimate goal or objective. As a versatile thinker, you will find yourself less likely to become stuck in a rut of indecision and just spinning your wheels. When you deny yourself to be versatile in your thinking, you are, in essence sabotaging your own efforts, falling short of goal after goal after goal. It's an unnecessary dilemma, but not at all an uncommon one. More often than not, it will take a vantage point other than your own to realize and understand why your current path isn't working.

There's A Success Story In You, Waiting To Happen

Modesty is cool, but don't be afraid to give yourself some credit. Everyday, a surprising number of individuals, just like you, go out and tackle an objective with focused ambition, success and gratification, never even considering the possibility of failing.

Ironically, those fortunate enough to achieve what others may view as extremely difficult, or virtually impossible were never told, it couldn't be done. It's amazing how something that simple can make a big difference. If your mind listens to the crowd noise of negative and discouraging intent, breaking the cycle of self-doubt and moving beyond perceived limitations will likely never cease. As peculiar as it sounds, society seems acutely sensitive to the prospect of self-doubt and the reasons why something can't be done, taking even greater stock in the likelihood of failure over success.

I. M. A. R.
INSPIRATION + MOTIVATION + ACTION = *RESULTS*

This is a fundamental equation, yet the most powerful formula to start you on a pathway to achievement, which can ultimately lead to success, once applied toward any endeavor. This is a formula to know and apply to all of your endeavors, no matter how great or how small.

I challenge you to try it and put it to the test. Most importantly, do whatever it takes to get started.

Whats Holding You Back? Do You Know?

Do you realize what you think, what you say, what you do matters? You have the capacity to offer tremendous contributions, no matter how minuscule you feel they are. To someone else, they're life changing. Maybe you don't want to admit to any of these on the list below, but until you do, nothing is going to change. Each one of these listed below are very real. Whatever the ruling factor, or combination of factors are that's putting the breaks on your efforts or opportunities will need to identified, accepted and confronted head on. Once you've done this, being as honest with yourself as possible, place your mind on forging a strategy to defeat every factor that has impeded your ability to move forward.

Is It Self-Confidence?
If your self-confidence has never been fed, it will never grow. It's a fundamental development process that you must experience. The easiest way to start this process is by placing yourself in the company of likeminded and supportive individuals. There will come a time when you will have to dip your toe into the water, so to speak. You will, at some point need to move from a spectator to a participant, placing yourself

somewhere closer to the action of your goals, allowing them to become nurtured, and ultimately realized.

Is It Motivation?
There has to be a point of interest great enough to move you into action directed toward a goal. Don't just exist… LIVE!

Is It The Lack Of Knowledge?
You'll have to have some idea of what steps it takes to achieve whatever your goal is. It's important to ask questions and do some active research. You owe it to yourself to know enough to get a clear idea of the complexities of what it is you want to achieve. Other times you may be compelled, or necessity dictates to jump right in and learn as you go. Later on I'll discuss three personal endeavors which I had no prior knowledge, or related skills. My approach to all three was to jump right in an learn as I go. I have no regrets for taking that approach, and as a result my overall knowledge, experience and the success milestones that came with it, increased tremendously.

Is It The Lack Of Opportunity?
Although some opportunities aren't always freely handed out, it is important to know that it's possible to create your own. I can personally attest that many of my opportunities resulted from the fact that I never felt that something couldn't be done. I only had to figure a way to make it happen. When opportunities weren't blatantly apparent, I had no choice but to create my own.

Don't Be Afraid Of Your Creative Mind

Your creative mind is just as qualifiable and legitimate as your intellectual mind. Heaven forbid, a creative thought slips out of our subconscious mind and spills over into our conscious mind for all the world to bear witness, judge and wonder. True, the creative mind can be unpredictable, scattered and disheveled at times, but what's cool about it is, it's *your* mind, and *yours* only. What's even more unique about the creative mind is, it may not always seem to rule with a sense of logic or reason, yet, what results is often genius. You should *never* deny or silence your creative mind, simply passing it off as trivial, or less significant. You possess it for a reason, and believe it or not, it's an important part of what makes you, *you*. Allow what is within your mind to come forth and flourish. Don't be afraid of it. Accept your creative mind for what it is and embrace it! Life in a world of rigid and predictable calculations can be very mundane, unoriginal and much less rewarding.

You Must Be Confident In What You Do

Discard all the emotional baggage and self-doubt that has held you back for whatever reason. Put away all the excuses of why you can't, and say, I can! Dismiss the self-defeating disposition that whispers inside your head, "What's the use?" If you've ever felt you were undeserving of a purposeful and personal agenda of achievement in life, rethink it now. Don't let ANYONE tell you, you can't, when you know you can. We all have our own lives to live and our own challenges to overcome. Yes, life can be challenging at times, but whatever you do, don't allow your own mind to defeat you, before you even begin.

Forming A Negative Opinion Of Yourself

Believe it or not, thinking negative about yourself can be fatal to your personal development. Here's why…

Whatever it is we believe about ourselves, we have a tendency to act it out. If we've been told that we will never amount to anything in life, some will adopt that opinion and impose it on themselves. In turn, their actions or non-actions may reflect accordingly in virtually everything they do. It can be a damning and pervasive disposition that threatens the very idea of success, motivation and achievement. You must empower yourself, by your own qualified authority, the power of positive thought and possibility.

The Importance Of Not Giving A Damn

In pursuit of your own aspirations, and keeping your flame lit, it's critical that you not give a damn about the harsh unsolicited views of those who doubt you and/or those lacking in their own track record of achievements or desire to pursue any.

You must never allow someone's opinion of you to negatively impact, or impede your efforts and/or desire to achieve. For your own sake, it's important for you to quickly arrive at the resolve of not giving a damn about those who are unfoundedly critical of you. Dismiss them and move on. It doesn't mean to be impetuous and intolerant of healthy and well-meaning constructive criticism. You just need to know which is qualifiable—something you can use to advance your efforts, and which is pure nonsense.

Keep Your Focus, Your Mind Will Love You For It

Keeping a clear focus means blocking out everything that distracts you. There are some who live a good portion of their lives focusing on the wrong things. Some choose to live in a world of bitterness, chaos and discourse, purely wasting their energy and potential. Under these circumstances it's virtually impossible to move forward with any qualifiable gains and no positive force to move you along. Whatever it is you desire, you have to want it so badly that it hurts. I remember a time when my goal was to become an accomplished jazz guitarist. It was something I wanted so badly, I practiced morning, noon and night, even falling asleep with my guitar just to wake up the next morning, still trying to obtain what I wanted so badly. It took drive, motivation and an unwavering focus. More than forty years later, I'm still at it.

Master Your Motivation

Stronger than any mind-altering drug, the power of motivation is real, and you must possess it.

With that being said, I strongly encourage you to make a concerted effort to be in the company of positive, creative and goal oriented individuals. The power of motivation can be triggered from within or by external factors, depending on your individual constitution. It's usually the strong-willed person who push themselves to achieve goal after goal and actually reach them. It's quite understandable that whatever your goal is, a direct path to completion may not always come to you crystal clear.

Of course you'll have some days when motivation is nowhere to be found. It's natural. In fact, it should be expected at times. Those are the times when it becomes expressly critical to maintain your focus on what you really want to achieve, not allowing your interests to wane, or give in to a false sense of complacency. Take advantage of the opportunity to reflect on what you've accomplished thus far, and what you still desire to achieve. I'll be the first to admit, I believe it's important to have an occasional moment of pause. No one can go full throttle all the time. Sometimes we need the white noise of nature.

Your Motivation Should Play Out Like An Action Packed Movie

Thrill seeking, adrenaline rush, high-speed car chases, explosions, the whole nine yards. Hang on for the ride! That's how it should go. Your motivation should hit you like a tidal wave, with *you* suddenly in the role as action hero of your own ambitions. The truth of the matter is, you'll never find anyone more suited for the role than YOU. Now, go and be a star!

Discovering The Untapped Potential Within You

Static electricity, as chaotic and random as it is, think about it. If it were harnessed and focused toward a given directive, imagine the potential. The untapped, forgotten or overlooked potential that dwells within you is very much like unharnessed static electricity. It's everywhere, all over the place, but at the same time, it's nowhere at all. It's all just a bunch of random, chaotic and unpredictable bursts of energy, until you focus it, and give it a purpose.

Maybe one day someone told you, you were really good at something. Maybe you discovered it on your own, but for whatever reason, chose to ignore or forget about it all together, allowing life to wear the once sharp edge of potential to a dull and less formidable opponent of day-to-day conformity and mediocrity. The latter seems the most prevailing, exemplified in the lives of a generous portion of the population. Everybody has potential to do new, great and undiscovered things. You have that very same potential within you. It's always been there. The truth of the matter is, you were born with it. You just have to realize it and rediscover it. I guarantee you, you'll find it, if you just look hard enough.

CHAPTER FOUR

MASTERING YOUR DESTINY

The definition of who you are may take years for you to author, but the destiny of who you are to be was written long ago.
—MAURICE JOHNSON

Your destiny is yours and yours alone. The journey that unfolds before each of us is individual and unique. Some may argue that our destiny is predefined. Perhaps so for those complacent within the boundaries of their comfort zones, but if you were to ask, could someone master and rewrite their destiny? The answer is—definitely yes! Start by evicting old notions and false ideas that what's born from your mind isn't worthy of pursuit. It's just not true. Take possession of as much of your own destiny as you can. Reclaim the *whole* you and realize that *you* are truly your own greatest asset. Start by waking up with the sun.

Don't let the morning escape you by allowing the afternoon to find you in bed. There is much truth to the old adage, *"The early bird gets the worm."* All too often I hear the words, I'm not a morning person. My advice to you is train yourself to be one. If you want to be successful, think successful. Start with the little things. Do NOT get up in the morning and log into an online game and suddenly find yourself at twelve-noon peering into a computer, tablet, cell phone or television screen while your thoughts, ideas and dreams become distant, vague and heaven forbid, insignificant and ultimately forgotten. Don't let it happen, because if you do this as routine, you're doing yourself a great disservice. Just think! There's a million other people out there transforming themselves into doers in the early morning hours. The question is, does that mean wake up in the morning and walk two miles? Perhaps. Does it mean jump out of bed and start penning ideas for a novel that's been stuck in your head, or begin writing a memoir? Could be, but the point I'm trying to make is for you to become one among those who ignites a spark of interest and remains faithful to it until it's completion.

20 SECRETS TO MASTERING YOUR DESTINY

1. Know What Inspires You

For quite some time I, like a thousand others faithfully post to social media, virtually on a daily basis. Over time there has grown an increasing sense of obligation on my part to post my daily mantras, words of encouragement or something simply to engage the minds of loyal followers. I'll admit, it's flattering when someone says they look forward to my posts as a source of inspiration while contemplating what their response will be for the next day. Sure, I can tell you to be inspired, get inspired, get off your butt and make something happen, but if it's not in you, nothing will happen. Somewhere within you has to be a spark, a glimmer of hope, a simple desire, or at least willingness to receive encouragement when it comes your way. Oddly, there are those who have become so conditioned to resist the remotest suggestion of expressing or accepting their own potential or individuality. For whatever reason, they are too afraid to test the waters of uncertainty, only relying on the predictable.

2. Realize That Somebody Out There Needs You

You may not realize it yet, but somebody out there needs some knowledge that you possess. Somebody out there needs something you do. Somebody out there needs something you have.

The last job I held was an advanced tech for a well-known telecommunications company after nearly eight years having worked in various capacities throughout my tenure. Being the type of person that I am, the personal gratification I had once felt as an employee waned terribly toward the end. On one particular day my own disenchantment suddenly became minuscule and insignificant after noticing a fellow employee who, by the look in her eyes, appeared to say she no longer felt like living. I've never seen that look before, but it was real and it immediately grabbed my attention and genuine concern. Something in her eyes moved me to deliberately intervene. It wasn't vanity, or the fact that I'm a good natured and gregarious person, but something deep inside told me to step into this person's life. After that, every day for the next few weeks I made it a point to say hello and strike up a conversation at every opportunity. It became important to me that our conversations and questions remained focused on her. My intent was to get inside her head and learn what she enjoyed most in life, her dreams, her goals and forgotten hopes. All in all, I simply wanted to distract her from herself. We all lived in the graduating stress of our jobs, and ultimately it took her life. She died of a heart attack, alone on the side of the road on her way home from work. The bottom line is that everyone wants to know there's someone out there who cares. During our brief acquaintance, a light came back into` her eyes. She was suddenly alive again.

3. Inspire Then Be Inspired

Sometimes I'll come across someone with noticeable drive and ambition. Although young in their endeavors and aspirations, I can plainly see their determination to achieve shine through. At some point in our conversation, they often intently share their heartfelt dreams with me.

What I've shared with those individuals, I'll share with you as well. Keep that spirit and amazing drive you have. You're going to do great things. All you need to do, is believe it. I know sometimes we want to hold back and hesitate, not quite following through. You're growing and testing the boundaries of your comfort zone. It's a natural process, and you'll soon step beyond particular thresholds in your life. You're on the right path and you *will* make it happen. Stay on your path.

4. Don't Let Life Steal Your Dreams

Don't wear your heart on your sleeve. At times your efforts will be wrought with emotion, near successes and what you may perceive as missed opportunities. If necessary, remove yourself from the presence of those who don't nurture your aspirations. Tune down the negative noise in your life. Free yourself from emotional baggage. These are the things that can suck the life right out of your desire to accomplish things.

5. Recognize Your Accomplishments

There comes a time when you have to give yourself some credit. Look back and think about what you've accomplished thus far. It might take a little study and self evaluation. It's easy to get so wrapped up in life that we fail to recognize ourselves. What seems a small accomplishment to you may very well be a huge accomplishment to someone else, so give yourself some credit.

Once you start recognizing some of your own past achievements, you'll begin to understand and believe that future achievements are possible as well.

6. Realize Your Value

If you want to accomplish anything, you'll have to believe this 100%. Don't back down if your mind, heart or someone else tries to tell you otherwise.

7. Don't Disqualify Yourself

Occasionally I'll come across someone who nullifies the very idea of cultivating any thoughts of independent endeavor. Move and advance in life by your own authority. It's important for you to understand that it doesn't take someone else, a degree, a high income or social status to validate you and/or your ideas. Throw that destructive mindset out the window.

8. Don't Hide Behind Your Ideas

Your ideas don't define you. It's quite the other way around. Sometimes you have to become bigger than the ideas you devised. I told that to a friend who was developing a brilliant, but complex product idea. He had been immersed in his endeavor for nearly twenty years, consumed by the complications of development and still without an entry to market date or year.

9. You Get To Write Your Own Rules

In a nutshell, you become the author of your own destiny. Sure, life, family, friends and strangers can offer tips, suggestions, insight and encouragement to help get you started, but where you take it from there is entirely your call. Take what you've learned from others, digest it, process it, mold it and reshape it until it works for you. When it comes to your future, your happiness, your purpose, and pursuing success driven goals, no one can navigate that journey like you can. Here's where you get to write your own rules.

10. Put Life In Its Place

At some point, you're going to have to level the playing field as you develop a mental survival strategy to help you stay upwardly mobile. All too often, life imposes, as if to deny us a fair shot at pursuing anything outside the realm of a day to day hustle and grind, just to keep the bills paid. It will become necessary to momentarily turn a deaf ear to a screaming late bill when you have no choice but to wait until the next pay period. At times life will indeed need to step aside and wait on you. The point I'm trying to make is, don't stress out when things don't happen in life when or how you want them to. There will be times when all you can do is keep your focus to stay on task and let the world move around you, always reminding yourself, your objective is just ahead.

11. Fear Of The Unknown Is Natural In All of Us

Most everyone has at least one goal they're afraid to go after. If that describes you, consider this. The person who is too afraid to try has already failed. From the most successful to the humbly ambitious, we all have some of the same fears to face. Although some can be kept at bay for a while, or terrifically avoided, yet from the most powerful person to the most vulnerable, we are all the same in that respect. It's perfectly normal to feel a sense of apprehension with something that is different and unfamiliar to us. It's nothing to be ashamed of. In fact, it's a part of the natural learning process as we explore something new and unknown.

12. Dismiss Distractions Whenever Possible

Right off the bat, I suggest you dial back the negative volume down to zero. What I really mean is, you'll need to deflect or do away with much of the distracting, counterproductive and emotionally draining energy that compromises your ability to focus. Start by controlling the urge to engage in highly addictive and endless social media comment streams involving politics, world affairs, race, religion, online games and the like. Whether you realize it or not, the social media platforms where these activities occur are strategically engineered to anticipate and evoke the most addictive behavior patterns of its users. Unfortunately, society has become the subject of an insidious experiment in pleasure and reward. Pleasure, being the content or activity while reward comes in the form of a gratifying like or follow. The most alarming fact is, it works. All the energy, ambition willpower that you possess has been usurped, redefining an increasingly docile culture's measure of self-worth, social acceptance and personal identity. It's an alarming and harmful assault on society as a whole, and it's only getting worse. This can be a daunting hurdle for some to overcome, but not an insurmountable one.

As you know, life is going to happen. We all experience our own set of unforeseeable and unavoidable distractions as the dynamics of day-to-day life unfolds. Sometimes it's those very things that are beyond our control we can approach with a different mindset.

13. Know When It's Time To Re-invent Yourself

We're all born with some type of unique innate abilities. Often times, specific attributes, skills or gifts can remain dormant for a lifetime if they're never called upon, envisioned or even realized. The same goes for goals and aspirations. For some, there comes a time when sheer survival becomes the supreme motivation and for others it's the overwhelming determination to stave off a lifestyle of complacency. Some decisions can remain suppressed when there's a family in tow. Maybe it's being cautious, careful or pragmatic, and for those very reasons a fuse can remain unlit. For me, after losing my tech job of nearly eight years then ultimately denied unemployment at age fifty-one, my future was immediately contingent upon some fast and critical decisions.

Music was the one mainstay that held its tenure during the bleakest of times and now it would become the central focal point as an independent career path going forward.

14. Surround Yourself With These Types Of People:

- Inspired
- Motivated
- Passionate
- Creative
- Positive
- Open minded

15. View Your Ideas With A New Set Of Eyes

Seek a different vantage point. You may be surprised to see a solution to what was once a problem, that you never saw from your singular vantage point. Maybe it's an idea that requires a lot of startup capital. Alternatively, startup capital doesn't always mean cold, hard cash or a pristine credit rating. Think and think some more. Creative, out of the box thinking has value too. Never overlook or discredit its potential.

16. Don't Isolate Yourself.
All Input Is Helpful, To A Point!

The reason I say this is because, eventually you're going to need somebody. It's so easy to isolate ourselves in our own comfortable private bubble for days, weeks and sometimes years while developing an idea. That self-alienation, nose to the grinding stone approach to things can at times lull us into a state of self-gratifying complacency, and at the same time feeding us a false sense of productiveness, processing and reprocessing our own unique thoughts one way or another, and then another. You can't always go it alone. You'll hear a range of opinions and suggestions, but at the end of the day, the final decision is yours. Not all input from a critique standpoint is meant to be discouraging. Don't shut the world around you completely out. Allow yourself to be open to healthy input from others.

17. Grow Your Inner Wealth

When I speak of growing your inner wealth, I'm not referring to monetary wealth, at least not directly. However, I am speaking of the wealth potential in every idea, endeavor and achievement directly related to your decisions and actions to make them happen. For every good seed that you plant, nurture and bring to fruition, another rung in the ladder to your overall success is firmly put into place. This repeated process gains you yet another foothold to move higher towards your goals, one step at a time. You may have already planted several good seeds toward your own inner wealth, and don't even realize it yet. Look back on your accomplishments that brought to you where you are right now, as you aspire to new goals and long awaited objectives. Believe it or not, it's all by design, contained within every good seed, (idea seed in this instance) that you plant, nurture and put into action. Do you see how that works?

18. Don't Misrepresent Yourself Trying To Be What You're Not

Somewhere in your makeup, your predisposition is what may not have yet been realized. What I'm getting at is, the *you* that you're supposed to be may be sequestered deep within your subconscious mind, waiting to come out. Sometimes, going through the motions of something long enough begins to feel like what is natural, when in reality it's simply familiarity, fueled by repetition. All too often people will live much of their lives within a cycle of familiarity and habit, succumbing to the idea that it's their own natural ability, what they do best, when deep inside they're saying, *"I don't know anything else."* This is typically the point where many will come to accept this is where the extent of their achievements begin and end. It's not true. Learning who you are can be a lifelong journey, but knowing who you are can be a lifelong adventure. Once the reality of knowing who you are comes into full view, and is fully accepted, your life begins. That's the point when you truly realize the world is *your* stage. It's when life has to play by *your* rules, with *you* calling the shots. That's the point when you take life and run with it.

When we live our lives in the shadow of who we think we're supposed to be, we fall painfully short of living an enriched, satisfying life with well deserved opportunity, achievement, reward and self empowerment. Really, it can happen. You just have to know and accept who you are, believe it and live it.

19. Don't Believe Your Ideas Aren't Worth A Second Thought

The fact of the matter is, with that kind of thinking you're doing yourself a great injustice. Don't disqualify, dismiss or nullify your ideas. There's value in them, but sometimes our own fears, apprehensions and self-doubt can cloud and even extinguish a good idea's ability to evolve, let alone flourish.

20. Be Prepared To Think Differently

Years and years of the same thought process yields the same result. At times, you'll have to trust what may not feel instinctive to you, in order to see yourself in a different light, or on a broader course. You would be surprised at the number of people who don't see their own potential, or a particular aspiration, until out of nowhere, an opportunity taps them on the shoulder, and a journey begins.

I've experienced them many times. Everything happens for a reason. I don't believe your progression through life happens through mere happenstance. Somewhere along the way your personal progress is the result of a deliberate action. Not always an immediate action. It may have occurred by virtue of someone you met, who is somehow directly or indirectly related to your interests. It could have been days, weeks, months or even years back. A connection may have evolved from within your own city, another state, or from half-way around the world. Somewhere there is a connection that ties us all within our unified interests or even needs. You only have to be receptive to it. Your mental preparedness and less inhibited action, and/or reactions all play an integral role in removing some of the barriers that can stifle an opportunity, dim the light of inspiration and ultimately sabotage your overall efforts to advance.

CHAPTER FIVE

THREE OF MY SUCCESS MILESTONES, AN INSIDE LOOK

The gestation period for a terrific idea is a lifetime.
—MAURICE JOHNSON

From a public perspective, my background is in music, jazz guitar in particular.

Upon arriving to Oklahoma City in 1985, shortly thereafter I formed a band. Over the years we became very popular, performing many events starting in the local Oklahoma music scene. Our tenure brought with it many performance opportunities including clubs, restaurants, major music festivals, television appearances, major recording artists concert openings, and ultimately our own record deal with a New York record label. Those were some truly exciting times and opportunities. But like the story of many bands, our's would succumb to an abrupt demise in 1993, just two weeks after performing as the opening act for another major recording artist of the time. It is from that experience I came to realize that it was time to reinvent myself. I poured myself into projects that I deemed worthy and worthwhile at the time. I was faithful and dedicated to bring each one of my endeavors to a successful resolve.

I was driven and burned with the desire to emerge successful at *everything* I put my hand to. The following are three examples that impact me to this very day. As you read you will get a glimpse of some of the steps it took to reach each of these success milestones.

D'LECO GUITARS

The History: In 1991 James W. Dale, (luither/guitar builder) and I co-founded D'Leco Acoustic Instruments. Together we designed, built and marketed exclusive, high-end handcrafted, arch top guitars.

Skill Sets:
Maurice Johnson - Guitarist, Graphic artist and Visionary, which in essence meant that I had a gift of gab, a risk-taker/marketeer and dreamer.

James W. Dale - An excellent carpenter and wood craftsman, who upon meeting me was engaged in his first attempts at building an arch top guitar.

Interesting Facts:
Arch tops are closely associated with jazz guitarists, e.g. Charlie Christian, Joe Pass, Wes Montgomery, George Benson, etc. They get the name from the subtle curved/arched top and back, similar to a violin or cello. In the guitar world, the handcrafted arch top guitar is what the grand piano is to the world of fine and expensive pianos.

What Brought Us Together
Fate perhaps, but in general terms, we were deliberately introduced by a mutual acquaintance.

What Sparked The Idea:
I've always been a visionary, able to see the broader possibilities of an idea. I was so impressed by James' early attempts building fine, handcrafted guitars and knew somehow the concept had to be scaled up. The challenge was to first recognize the market and figure out what needed to be in place in order to create a means of mass production. In this case, several things had to happen, thanks in part to fate and fast acting.

The Challenges:
- Create a unique and exclusive element of value.
- Establish legitimacy in the high end guitar industry.
- Legal representation.
- Gain the interest of a third party, major guitar manufacturer.

Result:
James Dale and I together reached several milestones.

Working closely with the family of legendary jazz guitarist, Charlie Christian, considered the father of the electric guitar, we secured the posthumous trademark of the Charlie Christian name. After designing a unique instrument, we licensed South Korean guitar manufacturer, *Samick Guitars* to mass produce our exclusive Charlie Christian *Solo-flight* line of three guitar designs.

After two years, we negotiated a special edition Charlie Christian guitar model with American guitar manufacturer, Gibson Guitars.

In 1996 one of our handcrafted guitars was featured in the *Smithsonian Institute* as part of the world famous, Scott Chinery, *Blue Guitar* collection.

I perform and record with one of my own guitar models to this day.

GIGORAMA SOFTWARE

The History:
In the mid 90s, I developed the once popular, Gigorama business management software for musicians.

Skill Sets:
None. I knew absolutely nothing about the software business, but I felt there was a strong need for Gigorama, and I was determined to make it happen.

Critical Attributes:
Ambitious, motivated, focused and a creative thinker with the ability to learn something entirely new.

What Sparked The Idea:
After reading an online review of my first book, The New Working Musician's One-Year Organizer, the reviewer stated, *"This would make a great software program!"* The wheels instantly started turning in my head.

Result:
I began to do research on what it entailed to develop a software program.

    I wrote a set of features that I wanted the software to do, designed a few user interface concepts and hired an advanced student programmer to write the code. Within a few months, Gigorama was born. At the time, there were very few software programs on the market to assist a working musician with a user-friendly approach. Gigorama helped musicians track their bookings, earnings, etc. It even printed out a contract with all the pertinent booking, earnings and client data for each event, and generated a financial summery for end of year tax filing.

    I built a website and allowed musicians to download a free, limited version, with the option to buy an unlock code to access the complete set of features. When musicians submitted their payment, I then generated a unique unlock code based on their first and last name, using another backend software that I had developed. When the code was entered, Gigorama would display the user's name on all screens and auto-populated it on all client contracts and forms when booking an engagement. I sold unlock codes for $69.00. Before long Gigorama was being featured and reviewed in various music trade magazines. My publisher offered me 25k to buy it, but I opted to license a version and negotiate a two book deal instead. Reason why is because I wanted to retain ownership. In order to make my counter offer work and still control my software, and sell it, I instructed my programmer to create a twin version of the software with added capability that allowed a user to uniquely communicate with each individual band member while the band leader/user maintained complete control. It was called, Gigorama, Virtual Network Edition. I sold unlock codes for $89.00 each. This move allowed me to still sell a version of my software while my publisher sold the original version. The contractual mechanism that allowed this to happen is called a *non-compete clause*. My publisher wrote me a 10k advance royalty check, I wrote two more books, and retained the rights to my software.

Conclusion:
Keep in mind, these were all concepts and marketing deals that I had never done before, with

no prior related business knowledge, but I was able to successfully pull it off.

PUBLISHED BOOKS AND ARTICLES

The History:
In 1996 I introduced "The New Working Musician's One Year Organizer" which was published by Mel Bay Publishing, who was very well known for their large assortment of music learning books, etc. This was the book that placed me on the path as a nationally published author.

Skill Sets:
Musician, Graphic artist ,Visionary and Risk-taker with an idea in tow.

What Sparked The Idea:
I started a band in the mid-80s. As humble as it was, the original idea came about seven years prior in 1989 after deciding to invest in my first attempt at self-publishing.

Interesting Facts:
I developed a musician's planner called, *Gig Monthly Planner for the Professional Musician* and pitched them to the local music store in my area. They were very supportive and bought a few to sell in their store. About a week later the store

contacted me and said the their jobber wanted to sell my books in four surrounding states. Naturally I was excited as he placed an initial order of four dozen. About a week later, on a Sunday morning I received a call from the jobber, requesting six more dozen in various colors right away. After that, I knew that I had tapped into a market that seemed to need this type of product.

The biggest challenge I faced was mass production and distribution. Without a broad distribution and working capital my market reach could only go so far. All the while, I clung to the thought that I had sparked the interest of a niche market and it was a viable idea, but eventually let the idea come to a rest after depleting my inventory.

It was a simple idea which basically amounted to a twelve month planner. Users had to fill in their own dates, which bought me extended shelf life. On the back of each calendar page was an area to log earnings and expenses. Users could also carry over year-to-date totals from the previous month. On the inside back cover was a basic entertainment contract. To help validate the contract, I met with the local musicians union and asked permission to include elements of their official contract, which they agreed to.

I always felt that it was an idea that had merit. After redesigning it, I submitted a prototype copy with a proposal letter to Mel Bay Publishing. The following week I received a letter of acceptance and contract from them. I was very surprised and naturally excited by the quick and positive response. Not only was it accepted, he stated that he intended to rush the production so then could release it at the Anaheim NAMM, National Association of Music Merchants, the largest music trade show in the industry.

Result:
It was that first publishing experience and the series of events that followed that transformed me into a published author several times over with four different publishers.

In the midst of it all, and because of that very first publishing experience, my confidence and knowledge increased, which lead to published articles in major industry magazines, and several nationally published books.

Step Out Of The Research And Development Department

I've drafted many ideas on the drawing board, and still do to this day, but this is what I learned throughout it all. I learned how *not* to be afraid to take off my lab coat, put on a business suit and introduce the world to my ideas. Some of you are deep in the research and development phase, after months and sometimes years, trying to work out all the bugs and *what if* scenarios to reach ultimate perfection before releasing concept version 1.0.

I understand that, and if this describes you, stay with it until your idea is finished and ready to introduce at whatever stage you deem as acceptable, but here's the kicker. Don't let your idea linger in a perpetual status of, *it's not quite ready yet*. Maybe it's a working prototype, suitable to engage in marketing or funding efforts. If your idea is service based, maybe you've honed it to a polished and workable set of actions, with all of the necessary accoutrements, if any. For those of you who have a fully developed, working and tangible idea that's waiting on you to give the final go ahead, but in *your* mind, it's never quite ready, I'm speaking to you. Time is of the essence.

Sometimes our perfectionism, uncertainty, fear of failure or even the fear of success can go on and on and on, keeping us in an endless research and development mode. Get on with it! Stop the procrastination and hesitating! For as long as you linger, procrastinate or remain in a holding pattern of excuses, you will never ever feel the gratification of achievement.

Other doors will open and new opportunities will present themselves. The question is, will you be ready when they do, or will you remain mentally stuck, working out or developing newly imagined flaws in the project you have now? Whatever endeavor you're engaged in, as you arrive nearer and nearer to its debut, you must resist the urge to stall, stifle and unknowingly sabotage your own efforts. Don't fight against yourself. Reserve that energy and thinking power and use it to your best advantage. You must be just as zealous in the release of your new idea to the world as you were throughout its development. At this point, your finished project has gained well deserved merit, and should shine like a star, and not go unnoticed like a faint whisper in a noisy, crowded room. You have a limited window of time to make an effective introductory impact. You will need to use the very same inspiration, motivation and energy that brought your this far when introducing your idea to the world.

Stay Excited And Motivated

Whatever it takes, get excited and stay excited. I know, it's easier said than done. It may take, and I highly advise this, finding someone who motivates you. Just as people who never know observe us throughout our lives. Ask yourself, what triggers your motivation or excitement about things. Give it some thought and find out what your personal motivational triggers are.

What Fear Whispers To Us

This is a stupid idea.

It's too complicated.

It's too simple.

No one needs this.

I don't have the money to do this.

I don't know what I'm doing.

It's just not quite ready yet.

How will I get the word out?

The competition is better.

I'm waiting for them to get back to me.

You Must Have Purpose

Purpose will wake you up early in the morning and make you stay up at night. Without purpose, halfhearted enthusiasm is about the best you'll have with anything while yielding the products of halfhearted results.

An Idea Worth Cultivating
Is Worth Pursuing

True, no doubt about it. If it was worth your time, energy and effort, cultivating an idea and bringing it to the surface of your conciseness then it deserves to be realized. Don't stay silent with your ideas bottled up inside. Talk about them. In fact, it's healthy, because the more you talk about them, the more excited and energized you will become. It will take that self-generated excitement and energy to keep you motivated throughout your endeavor. I highly recommend that you surround yourself with likeminded individuals.

Set Goals And Stick To Them!

Moving around from one goal or project to the next, and never completing any of them is a sure way to lose overall momentum. Sure, you're busy, but to what end. Lock on to your most passion driven, definitive goal, and complete it. By doing so, two things have occurred. One, you've placed another rung in your ladder to success and fulfillment and two, you're now able to free your mind in order to give your full attention to your next goal, thus gaining you momentum and proof that you can actually achieve, once you set your mind to it.

Keep Your Ideas Moving

Past accomplishments can fuel future accomplishments, just as past projects can fuel future projects. To keep things moving you will have to explore every nook and cranny of your imagination without questioning or second guessing yourself or your ideas.

Getting yourself and keeping yourself on a productive path will take some day-to-day planning and forethought. The less scattered your thoughts are each day, the more productive and creative your time can be. Optimize your personal productivity by getting in the habit of making a daily, *Today I Intend To…* check list for the following day, listing only the tasks that can realistically be accomplished within the course of one day. Make it a point to follow through with each one before moving on to the next. Something as simple as this can make a world of difference in increasing and tracking your daily productivity. Try it for a month and watch your productivity increase tremendously. Something as simple as dropping clothes off at the cleaners, or brainstorming the logistics of a new idea, it all boils down to developing a sense of organized thought and following through to completion.

Set Deadlines For Yourself
In essence, deadlines are nothing more than a series of short-term goals set with the intention of completing each one by a specified date. Once you've set deadlines and met them on time, your productivity will steadily increase along with your personal efficiency. You can

apply the following steps to enhance your own personal productivity and meet established deadlines:

- Routinely write a list of all your current projects.

- Number the items in your list, arranging them in order of importance and including deadlines for each. (Be sure to give yourself realistic time constraints).

- Decide, (only when necessary) which projects can be deleted and continued at a later date.

- Starting with the highest-priority item, complete each one before moving to the next.

The key to meeting deadlines is not to overwhelm yourself with too many projects at once. Organization will play a critical role in your overall rate of success. Think about it, if you're unorganized, with no established goals your personal productivity remains at a virtual standstill. It's about the most damning thing you could do to your overall personal progress.

Take Note Of Your Success Milestones

Have you ever thrown a stone into a pond and watched the ripples it creates? As the stone breaks the surface of the water, the entire pond is affected. Now, visualize that stone as yourself and all your efforts. The greater the effort, the larger the stone. If you can envision your efforts as ripples, you can begin to get a good understanding of how you can affect the scope of your own success. Some people excel faster than others only because of various circumstantial factors. It may be a matter of economics, geographic location, resourcefulness, or sheer determination. In truth, we all start out with the same success potential. Give yourself credit and don't disqualify your achievements.

Take into account the success milestones you've already reached. In fact, write them down. No matter how small, they all count in the big picture. Understand that it's okay to give yourself credit for your successes. They're yours, you earned them. Even if they were never recognized publicly, the important thing is that you accomplished them. So now, as I mentioned earlier, write them down. Grab a notebook or create a text document on your computer or tablet and title it, MY SUCCESS MILESTONES. You don't have to do this in one sitting. Add them as they come to mind. List and number every accomplishment/success milestone you can think of, no matter how small or how long ago it was. The reason I'm having you do this is because I want you to recognize, accept, qualify and take ownership of the successes you may not have given a second thought. You must get out of the habit of marginalizing your successes as if they never happened.

Once you've documented a fairly decent account of past success milestones, continue documenting them from here on out. In essence you're building a journal or success resume. It gives you concrete proof that you *can* be successful. Not only does it allow you to see your incremental success, but over time, you will begin to see your strong points as well.

Closing Thoughts

We all need an advocate. This is especially important for those in need of encouragement, someone who will stand with us, and behind us when no one else will. Every new life experience brings with it a certain level of apprehension and anxiety as we step outside of our comfort zone. Believe me, I've had my fair share, and I'm sure, many more to come. These are natural feelings that some refer to as growing pains.

Once you come to realize that great power resides within you, the power to create, formulate workable concepts and achieve is a formidable force. By your own authority, your own power and unyielding determination, grant yourself the right to cast aside your fears, self-doubts and hesitation and move forward, because it's *your* time now. No one else holds this power and ultimate authority but you. The only prerequisite is your heart and mind have to agree.

About The Author

Milwaukee born jazz guitarist, Maurice Johnson first gained notice in 1985 shortly after forming the Oklahoma City based, *After Five* band. Over their career they shared the stage with a host of major recording artists, including George Benson, Nancy Wilson, Al Green, Jennifer Holiday and many others. In 1991 the group signed with a New York label and released their debut Expressions album. After a nearly ten-year stint they would ultimately disband.

In the early 90's Maurice co-founded D'Leco Guitars, building and marketing handcrafted arch top guitars. They also designed and licensed an exclusive line of Charlie Christian guitar models to American manufacturer, Gibson Guitars and Samick Musical Instruments in Korea. The subject of many trade magazines and news stories, a D'Leco guitar was on display at the Smithsonian Institute among the exclusive, Blue Guitar Collection.

Between 1996 and 2003 Maurice authored three nationally published music related books with Mel

Bay Publishing, Mix Books and Artist Pro Press. Titles include, The New Working Musician's One Year Organizer; Build and Manage Your Music Career and Gigorama. During this time he would develop the popular windows based, Gigorama software.

Today Maurice is an Independent Recording Artist, Published Author with over twenty titles to his credit, and the founder of **SelfPublishMe**, *Publishing Consulting and Book Design for First-time and Independent Authors*.

Maurice Johnson is available for speaking engagements, consulting, interviews, etc. If you would like to submit a query, send an email to: mauricejohnson8@icloud.com

Five **Important** *Goals for This Month!* _____

1. _____
2. _____
3. _____
4. _____
5. _____

Notes: _____

_____

_____

_____

_____

_____

_____

_____

Five **Important** *Goals for This Month!* _____

1. _____
2. _____
3. _____
4. _____
5. _____

Notes: _____

_____

_____

_____

_____

_____

_____

_____

Five **Important** *Goals for This Month!* _____

1. _____

2. _____

3. _____

4. _____

5. _____

Notes: _____

_____

_____

_____

_____

_____

_____

_____

Five **Important** *Goals for This Month!* _____

1. _____
2. _____
3. _____
4. _____
5. _____

Notes: _____

_____

_____

_____

_____

_____

_____

_____

Five **Important** *Goals for This Month!* _____

1. _____
2. _____
3. _____
4. _____
5. _____

Notes: _____

_____

_____

_____

_____

_____

_____

_____

Five **Important** *Goals for This Month!* _____

1. _____
2. _____
3. _____
4. _____
5. _____

Notes: _____

_____

_____

_____

_____

_____

_____

_____

Five **Goals** *for This Month!* _____

1. _____

2. _____

3. _____

4. _____

5. _____

Notes: _____

_____

_____

_____

_____

_____

_____

_____

Five **Important** *Goals for This Month!* _____

1. _____

2. _____

3. _____

4. _____

5. _____

Notes: _____

_____

_____

_____

_____

_____

_____

_____

Five **Important** *Goals for This Month!* _____

1. _____

2. _____

3. _____

4. _____

5. _____

Notes: _____

_____

_____

_____

_____

_____

_____

_____

Five **Important** *Goals for This Month!* _____

1. _____
2. _____
3. _____
4. _____
5. _____

Notes: _____

_____
_____
_____
_____
_____
_____
_____

Here's more from *Maurice Johnson*

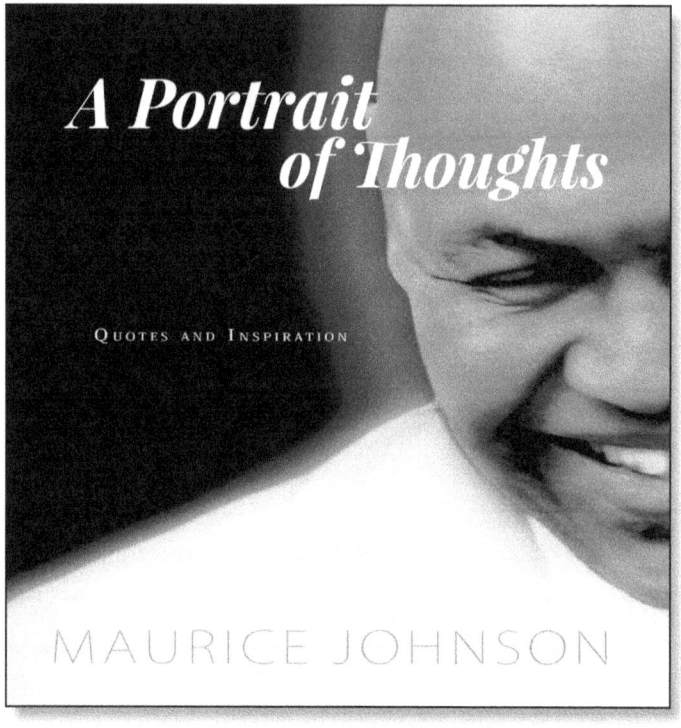

A PORTRAIT OF THOUGHTS *Quotes and Inspiration*

8.5" x 8.5" **Coffee table size print version**

OTHER MAURICE JOHNSON BOOKS

BREAKING INTO THE MUSIC BUSINESS
AS A LOCAL INDIE MUSIC ARTIST *(Book Series)*

BUILDING YOUR MUSIC CAREER

THE WORKING MUSICIAN'S ONE-YEAR
TIME and MONEY ORGANIZER

THE WORKING MUSICIAN'S ONE-YEAR
BOOKING and EXPENSE LEDGER

Maurice Johnson's GUITAR CHORD DIAGRAMS

Maurice Johnson's GUITAR NECK DIAGRAMS

The Indie Artist's Music and Lyrics Songwriting Journal

A Stolen Moment and A Hot Cup Of Coffee Writing Journal

A Stolen Moment and A Cool Glass Of Wine Writing Journal

I Write Music Therefore I Need Staff Paper

AN AMERICAN JAZZ ARTIST SERIES Writing Journal Vol. 1, 2 and 3

THREE GREAT WORDS 30 Day Writing Challenge (Activity Book)

DREAMS Writing Journal

THE FILM ACTORS AND EXTRAS CASTING CALL NOTEBOOK

A PORTRAIT OF THOUGHTS, *QUOTES & INSPIRATION*

A PORTRAIT OF THOUGHTS *(Square Coffee Table Format)*

Also available on Amazon!

Visit: www.mauricejohnson.com

www.ingramcontent.com/pod-product-compliance
Lightning Source LLC
Chambersburg PA
CBHW072210170526
45158CB00002BA/536